# The GIANT ANIMALS Series™

# Manatees

Marianne Johnston

The Rosen Publishing Group's
PowerKids Press™
New York

Published in 1997 by The Rosen Publishing Group, Inc.
29 East 21st Street, New York, NY 10010

First Edition

Book Design: Kim Sonsky

Photo Credits: Front and back cover © D. R. & T. L. Schrichte; p. 4 © D. R. Schrichte; pp. 5, 7, 10, 13, 16, 17, 18, 21 © Robert Rattner; p. 9 © Mark Newman/International Stock; p. 14 © D. R. & T. L. Schrichte.

Johnston, Marianne.
    Giant animals. Manatees / Marianne Johnston.
        p.    cm. — (Giant animals)
    Includes index.
    Summary: Introduces the physical characteristics, habits, and natural habitat of the manatee and examines the factors that threaten its survival.
    ISBN 0-8239-5146-4 (lib. bdg.)
    1. Manatees—Juvenile literature. [1. Manatees] I. Title. II. Series.
QL737.S63J64 1996
599.55—dc21                                              96–46607
                                                            CIP
                                                            AC

Manufactured in the United States of America

# CONTENTS

# WHAT IS A MANATEE?

A manatee is a large, gentle animal that can live in freshwater or saltwater. Even though they live in the water, manatees are **mammals** (MAM-els) just like we are.

Manatees live in shallow **coastal** (KOHS-tul) waters near the ocean. Sometimes they live in rivers and natural springs.

In the United States, manatees live in the waters of Florida and southern Georgia. Manatees can live to be 60 years old.

◄ Manatees like to swim along the bottom of rivers, looking for food.

# WHAT DO THEY LOOK LIKE?

Most manatees are about nine feet long and weigh about 500 pounds. But some can be as long as thirteen feet and weigh as much as 3,000 pounds! Female manatees are usually bigger than the males. The manatee's large, grayish-brown body looks kind of like a seal's body. Their skin looks smooth, but it actually feels like pebbles in wet sand at the beach.

Manatees have two flippers, just like whales do. Each flipper has three or four large fingernails. The manatee's huge, flat tail acts like a paddle. A manatee also has whiskers on its nose!

A manatee has fingernails, ▶
just like we do.

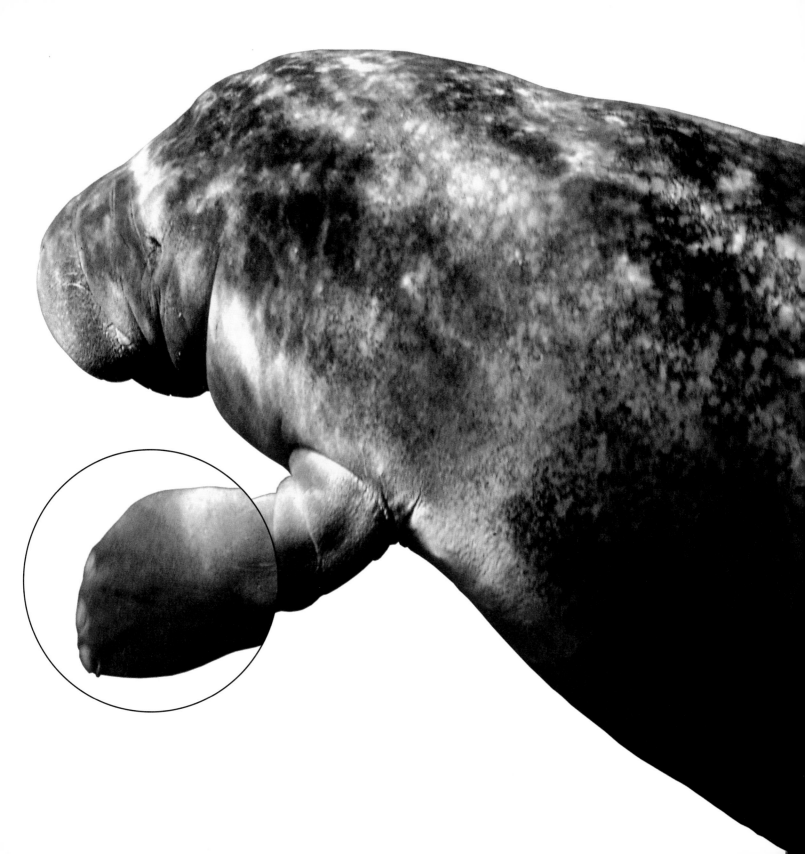

# DIFFERENT KINDS OF MANATEES

There are three kinds of manatees: Amazonian, West Indian, and West African. The Amazonian manatee lives only in freshwater.

West Indian manatees can live in both freshwater and saltwater. In the United States, they live around the states of Florida and Georgia. The West Indian manatee also lives off the coast of South America and in all areas of the Caribbean.

The West African manatee lives in the coastal waters and rivers of western Africa.

Manatees live in shallow water near land. ▶

# HOW DO THEY ACT?

An animal as big as a manatee might seem scary at first. But manatees will not hurt you. They are even shy around people.

Manatees swim slowly through the water, at about two miles per hour. They spend a lot of their time eating water plants.

Manatees are playful, too. Sometimes they play the game "Follow the Leader" with each other. Two or three manatees glide through the water, diving and moving in the same direction as the leader.

Manatees like to swim together as they move through the water.

# MANATEE SENSES

Manatees have small eyes but they can still see things that are far away. Instead of ears, manatees have two very small openings on the sides of their heads. Still, manatees can hear very well.

Mothers and their **calves** (KAVS) need to have good hearing because they make noises, like squeaks and squeals, to keep track of each other.

One of the most important senses for a manatee is touch. Mothers and their calves often touch each other.

A manatee's ears are so small you can barely see them. ▶

# MANATEES MIGRATE

During the winter, manatees tend to **migrate** (MY-grayt) from colder coastal waters to warmer **inland** (IN-lend) rivers and springs. They also gather near power plants, where the water is warm.

During the summer, some manatees move to the coast of Alabama. A few have even gone as far north as Virginia. That's about 800 miles from Florida. That's a long swim!

◄ Manatees have to migrate to warm water during the winter.

# WHAT DO MANATEES EAT?

Manatees are **herbivores** (HER-beh-vohrs). That means they only eat plants. They eat all kinds of **vegetation** (VEJ-eh-TAY-shun) found in the water, such as the **water hyacinth** (WAH-ter HI-uh-sinth), **algae** (AL-jee), and turtle grass.

Most manatees eat 100 pounds of food a day. This means they have to spend most of their day eating. A manatee's teeth wear out quickly because it eats so much. But when its old teeth fall out, new teeth quickly grow in to replace them.

The water hyacinth is one of the manatee's favorite foods. ▶

# YOUNG MANATEES

When they are born, baby manatees are about four feet long and weigh about 60 pounds. Most human babies only weigh about seven pounds when they are born.

Most West Indian manatees are born during the spring and summer. Females have babies about once every three years.

Newborn manatees can swim right after they are born. The calf stays with its mother for two years. It learns about what to eat and where to migrate to find warm water.

◀ Manatee calves get their mother's milk from a spot under their mother's flipper.

# MANATEES AND HUMANS

Humans can be very dangerous to manatees. Many manatees die because they are hit by boats that are driven by people. Some die from eating fishhooks and other garbage left in the water by humans.

But not all contact with people is bad. Manatees live safely at zoos and **aquariums** (ah-KWER-ee-ums). They also live in protected wildlife parks where visitors can go to see them up close and learn about them.

Baby manatees are being raised in aquariums by humans who want to help them. ▶

# ENDANGERED SPECIES

Manatees are an **endangered species** (en-DAYN-jerd SPEE-sheez). They might become **extinct** (ex-TEENKT) if they are not protected. The number of manatees has dropped over the years. Today, only about 2,600 West Indian manatees are left in the United States.

If coastal and river waters become **polluted** (poh-LEW-ted), manatees will have less space in which to live and grow. But people are now trying to protect manatees. In Florida, it is against the law to hurt them. Manatees' homes must also be protected so we can continue to enjoy them and learn about them.

# GLOSSARY

**algae** (AL-jee)  A water plant with no roots, stems, or leaves.

**aquarium** (ah-KWER-ee-um)  A place where fish, water animals, and water plants live and can be visited.

**calf** (KAF)  A young animal.

**coastal** (KOHS-tul)  Near or around the shore.

**endangered species** (en-DAYN-jerd SPEE-sheez)  A kind of animal that has very few of its kind left.

**extinct** (ex-TEENKT)  When a certain kind of animal does not exist anymore.

**herbivore** (HER-beh-vohr)  An animal that only eats plants.

**inland** (IN-lend)  Land that is away from the water's edge.

**mammal** (MAM-el)  An animal that is warm-blooded and gives birth to live young.

**migrate** (MY-grayt)  When animals move from one area to another.

**polluted** (poh-LEW-ted)  When an area is filled with garbage and waste.

**vegetation** (VEJ-eh-TAY-shun)  Plant life.

**water hyacinth** (WAH-ter HI-uh-sinth)  A flowering plant.

# INDEX